# Paisley Patterns

## AN INTRICATE ADULT COLORING BOOK

A Division of Hart House Media LLC
Austin, TX

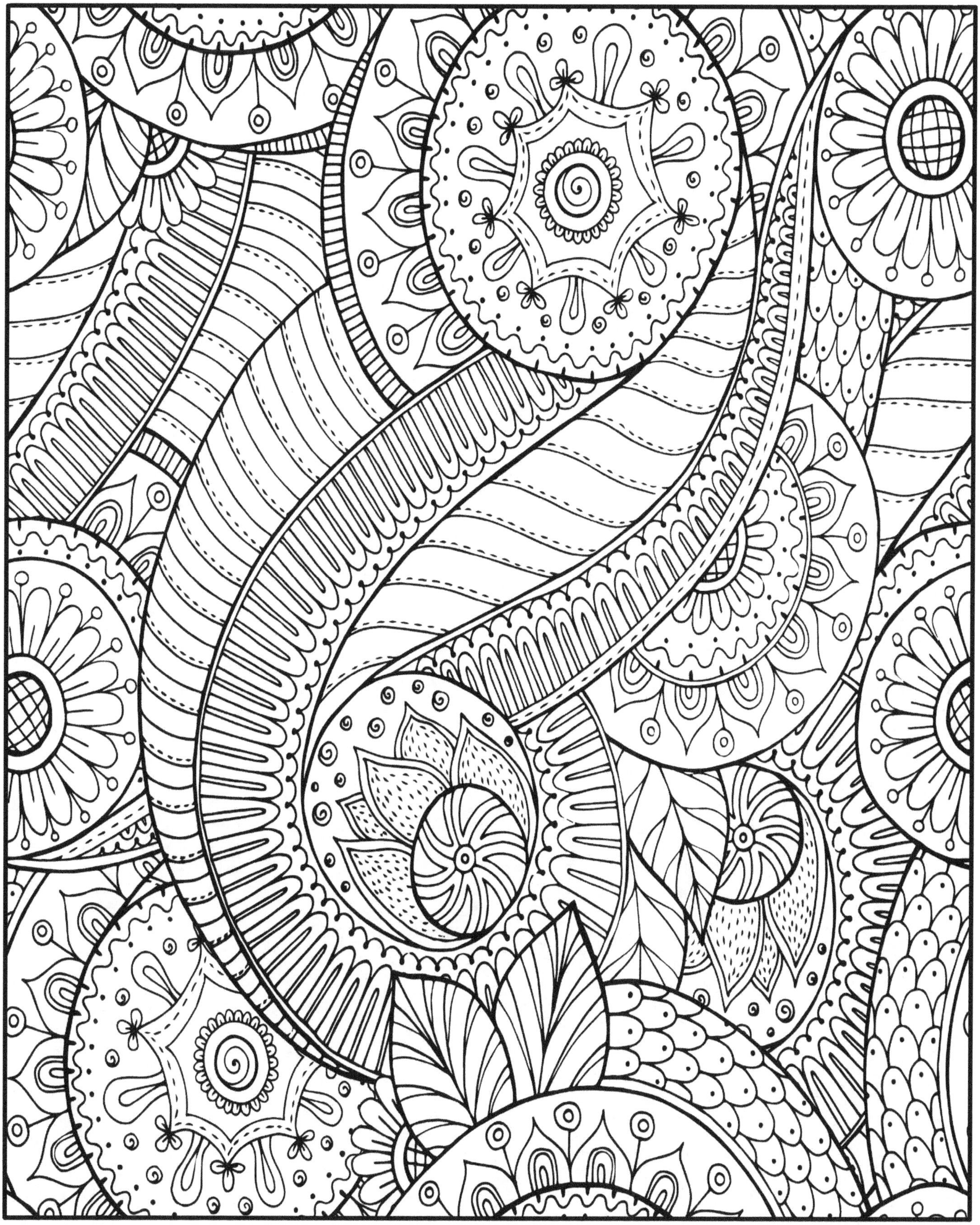

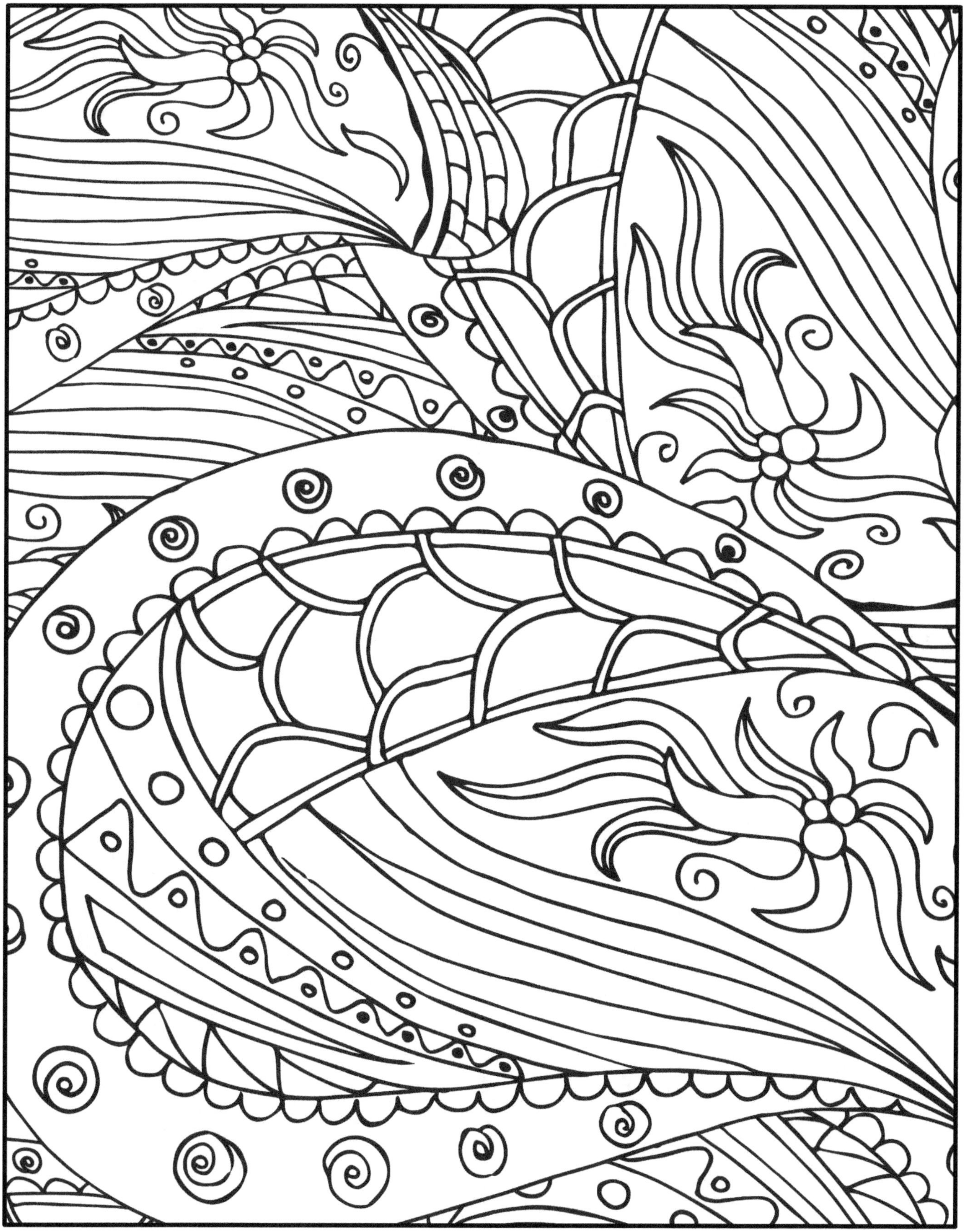

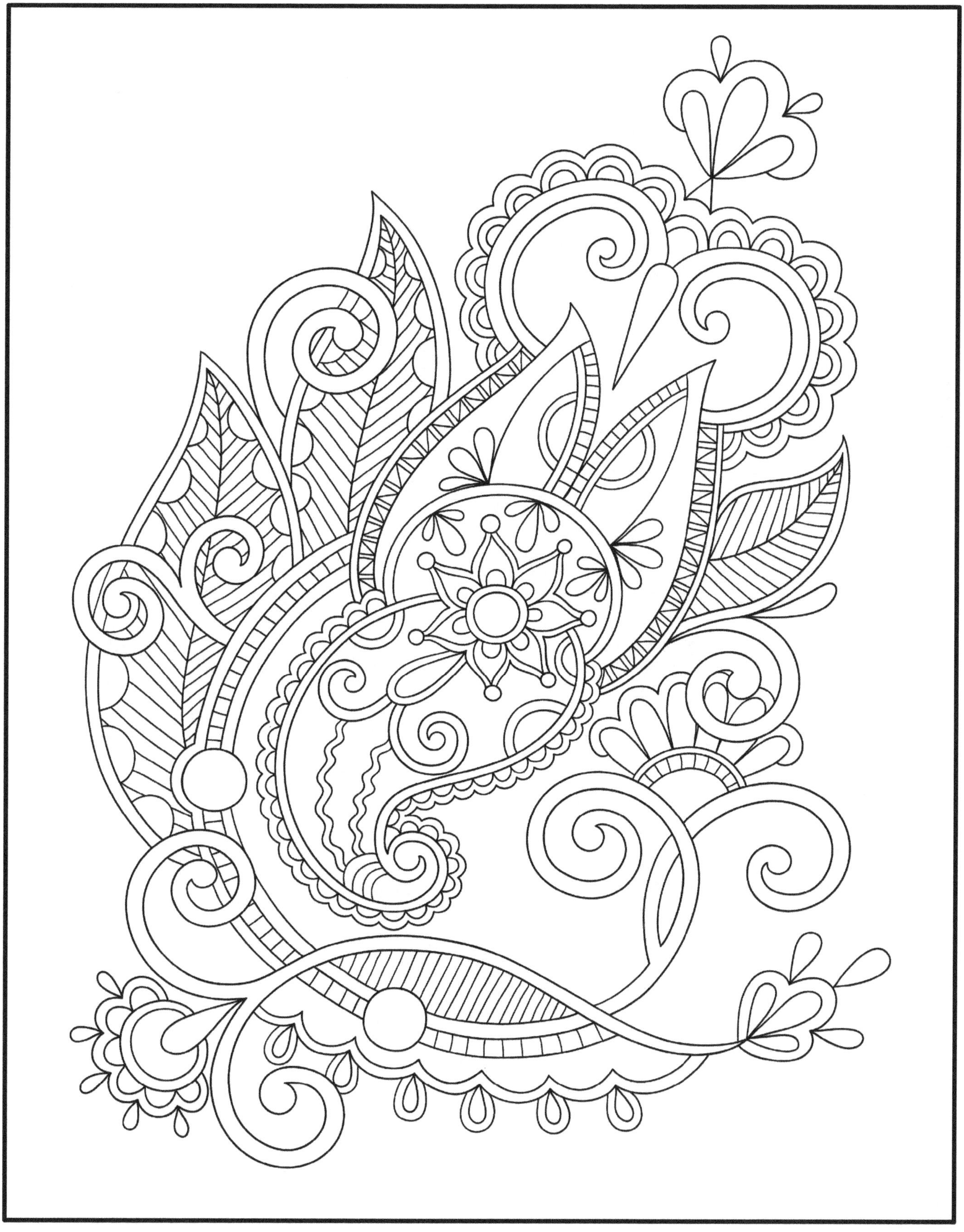

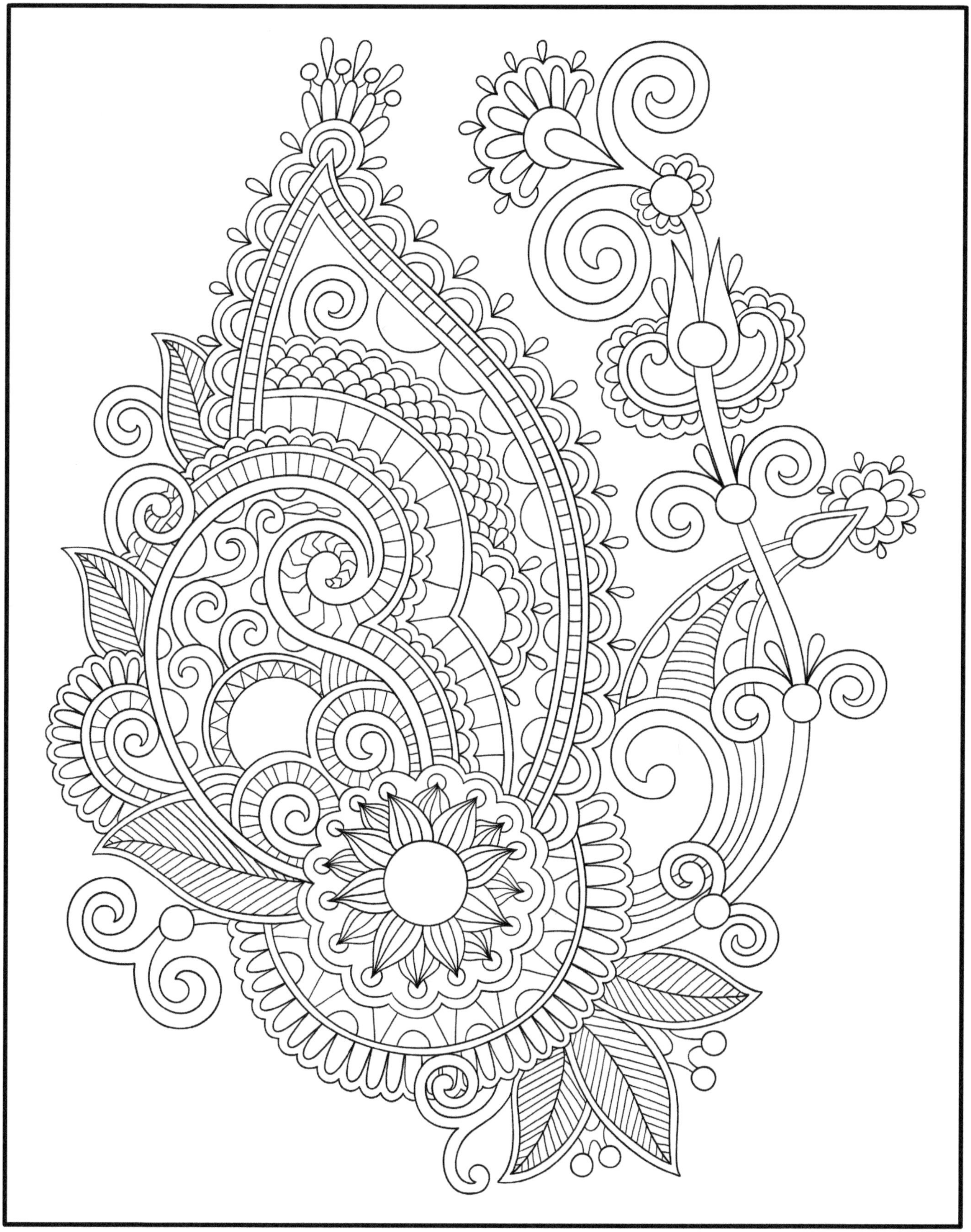

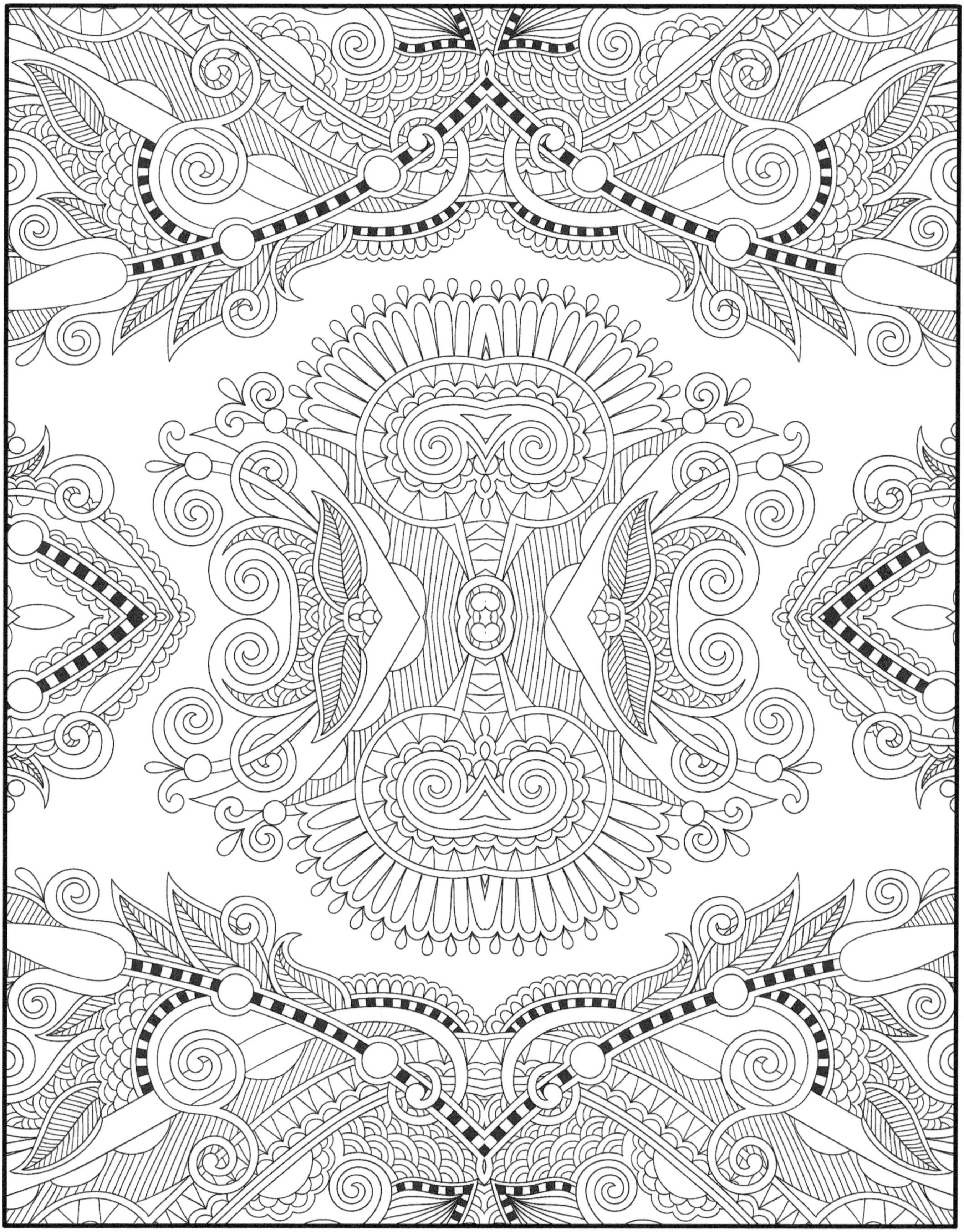

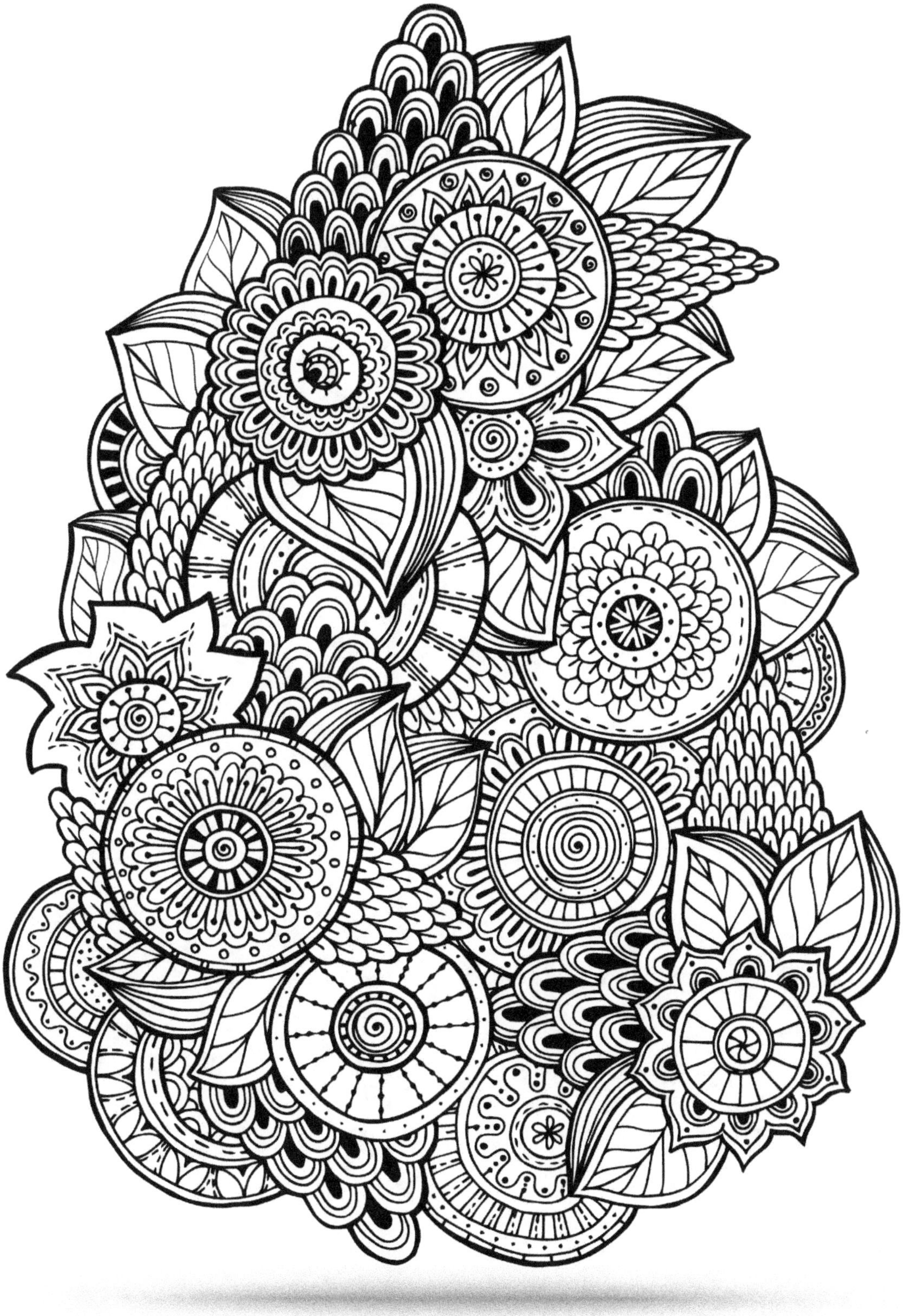

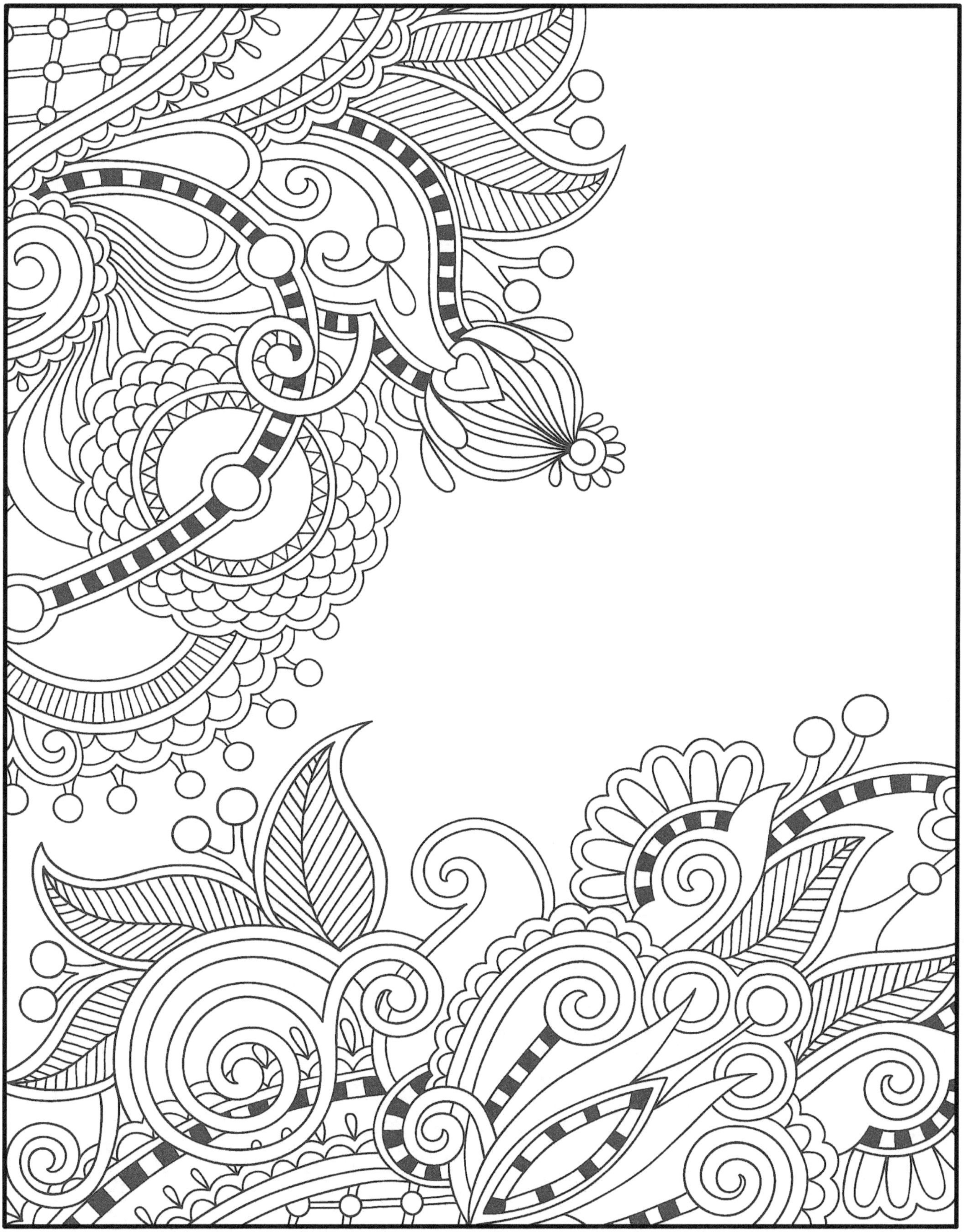

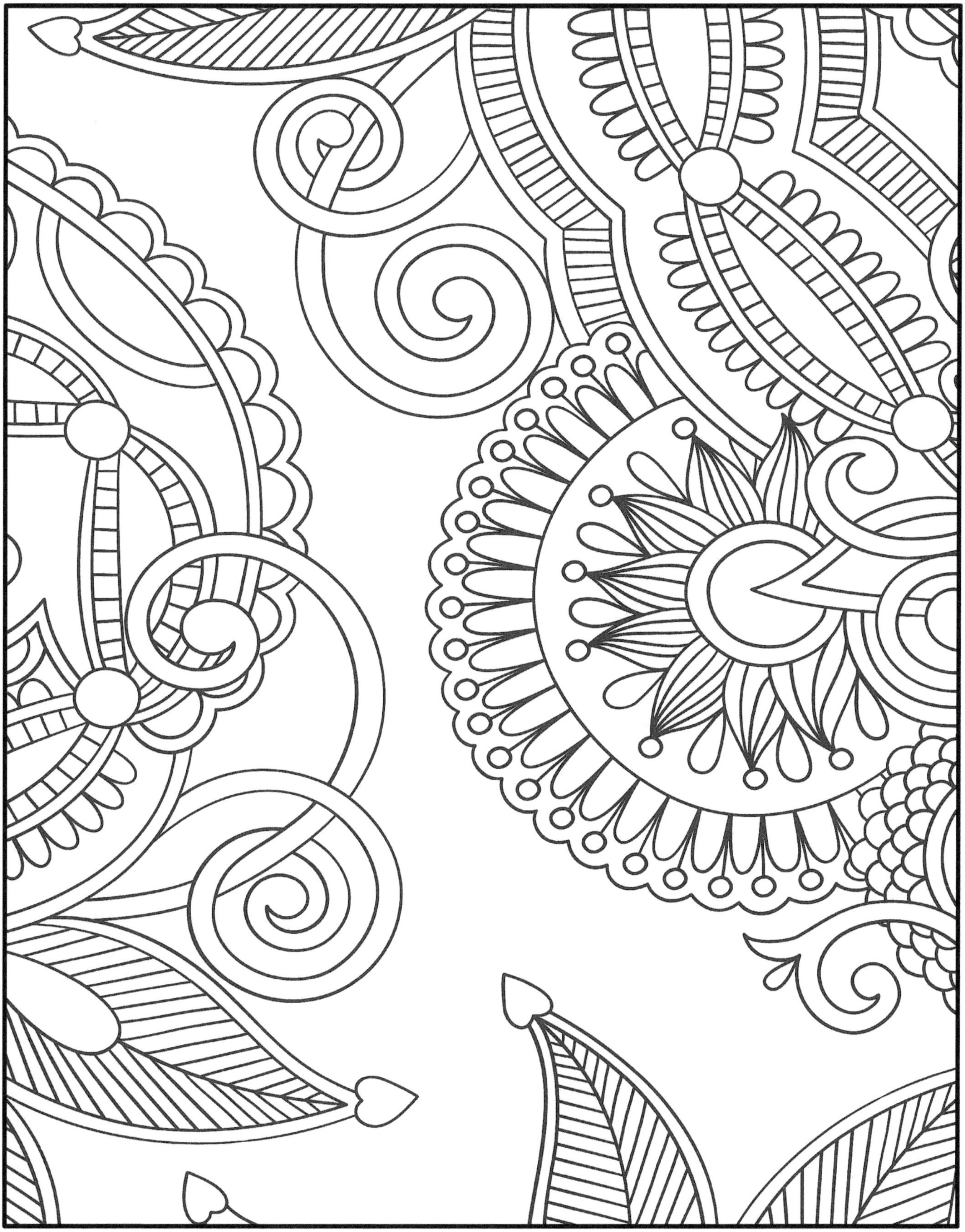

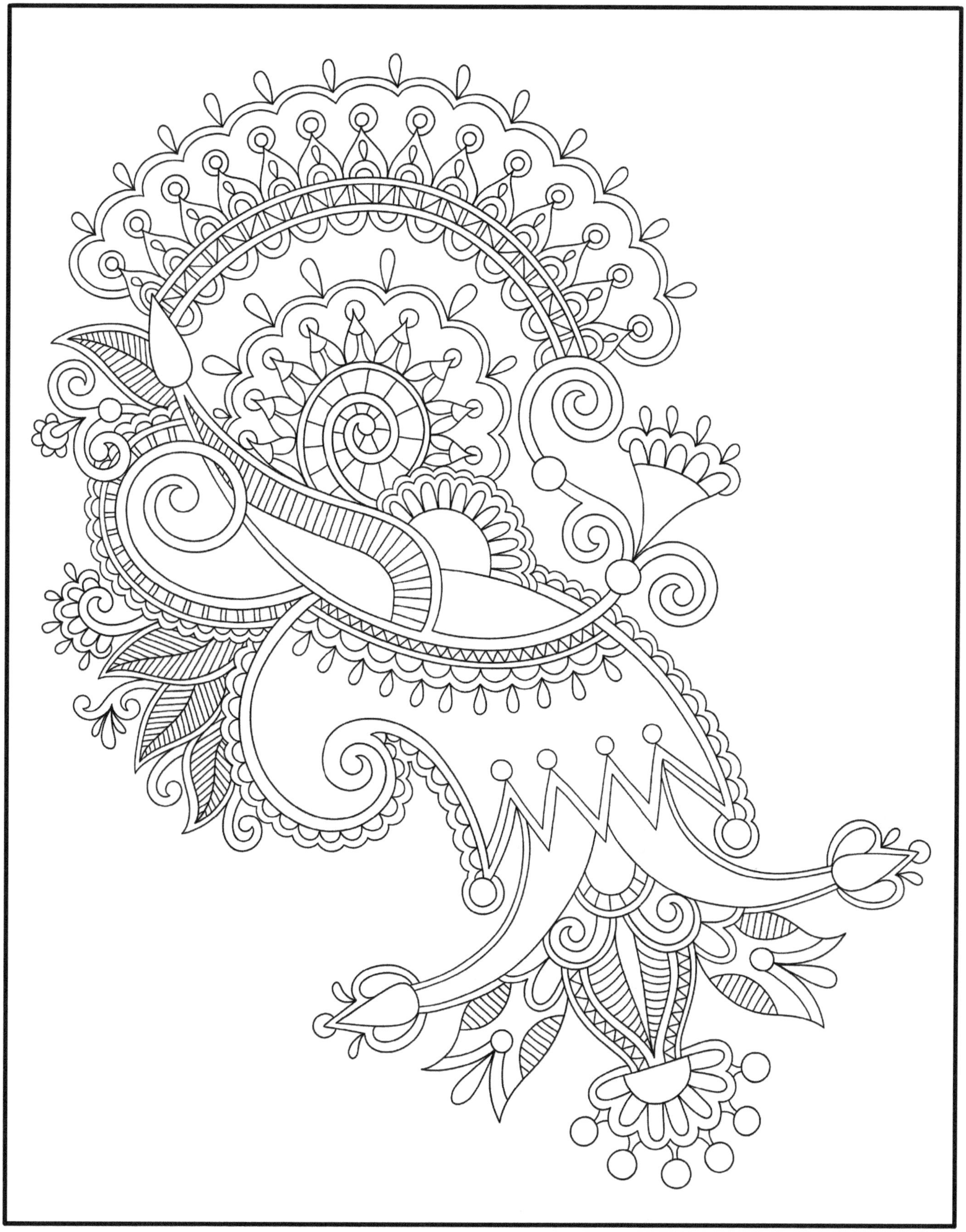

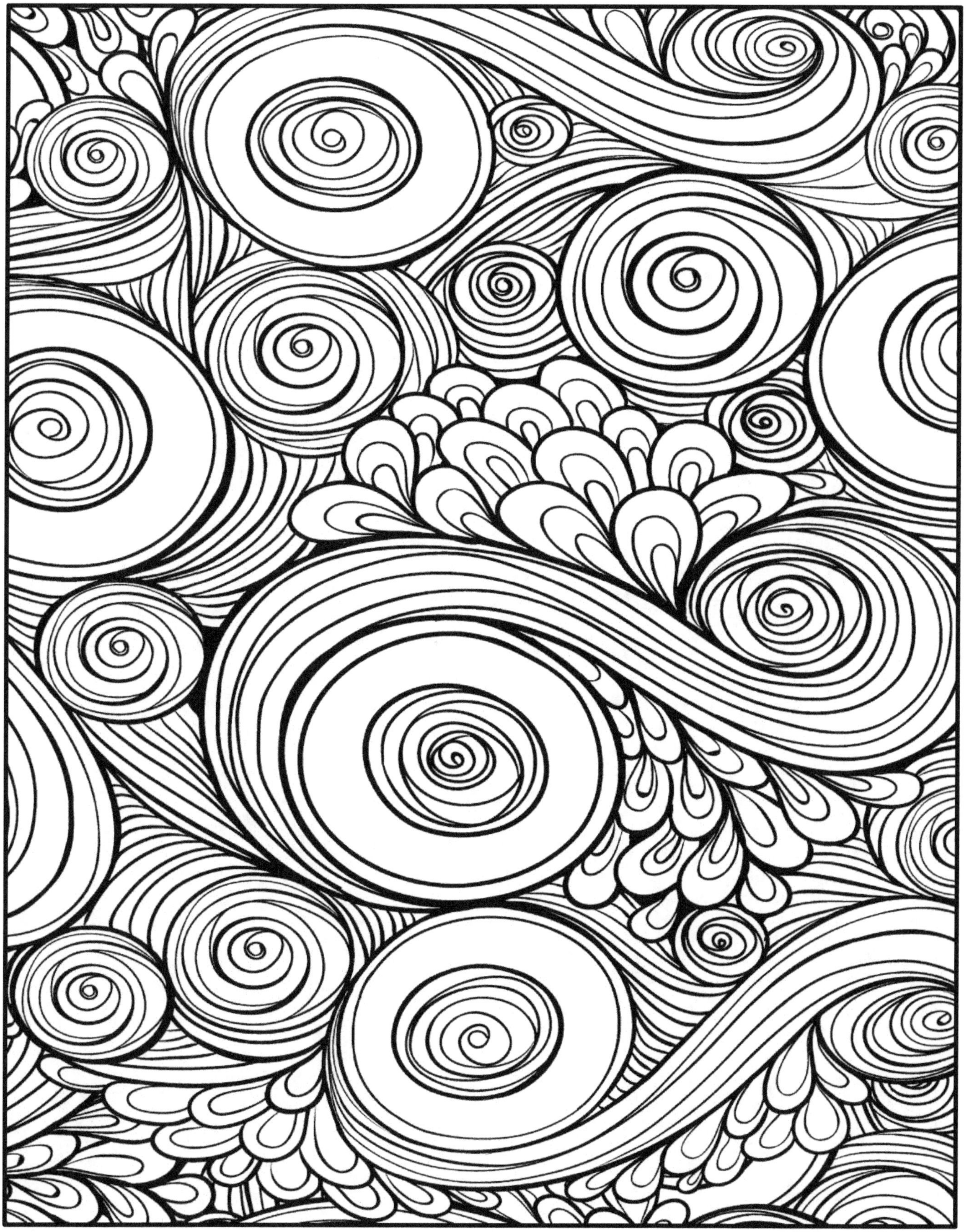

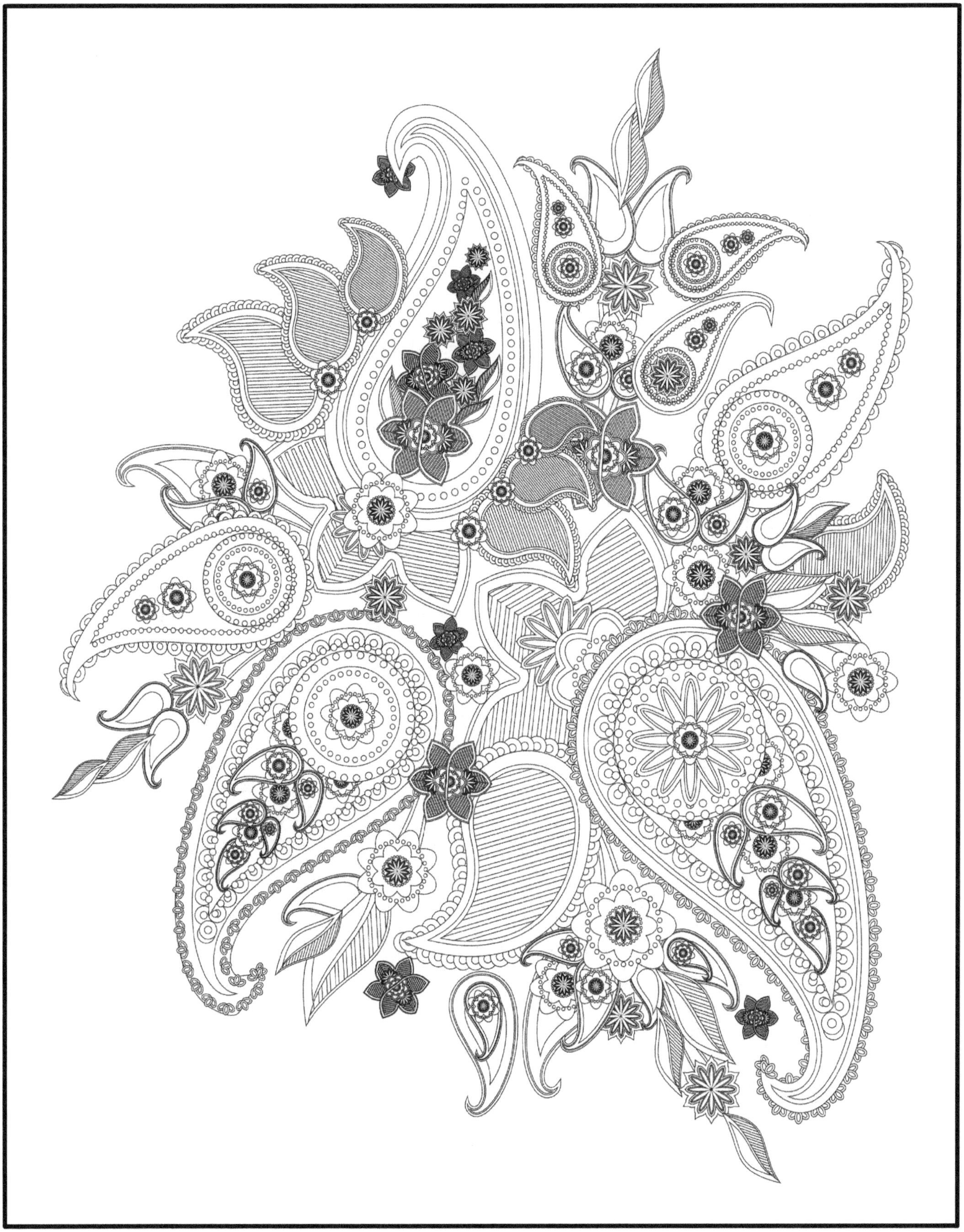

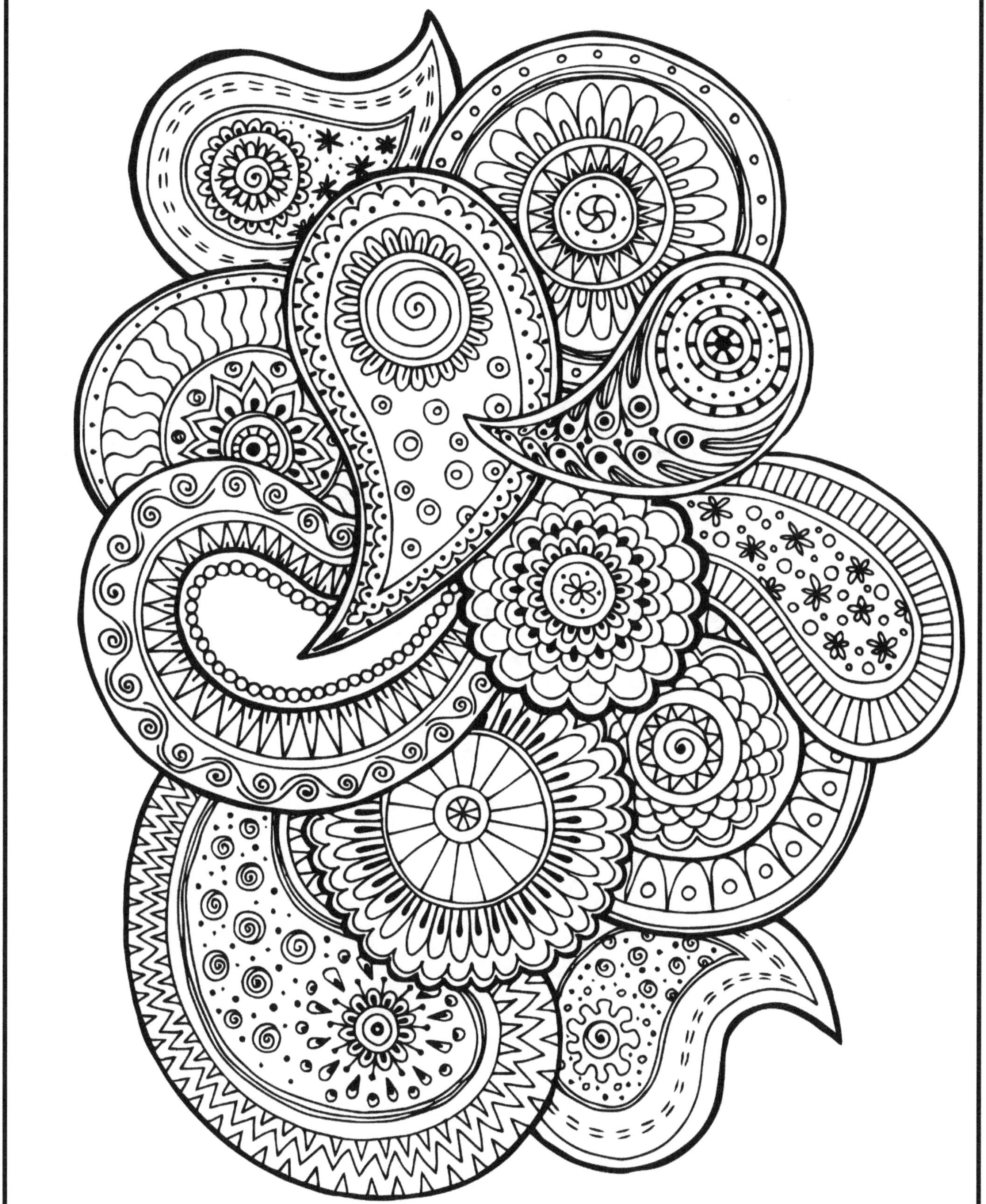

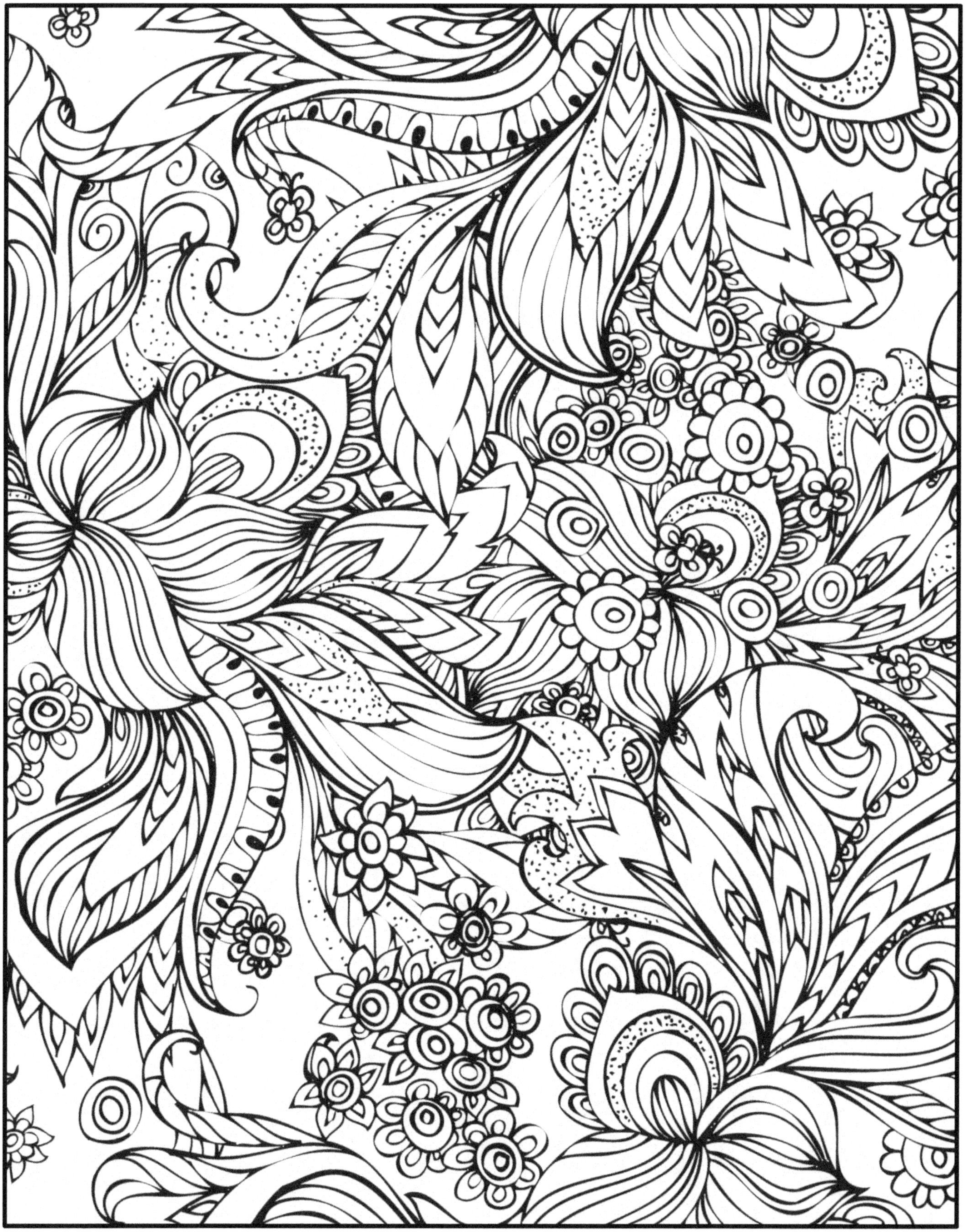

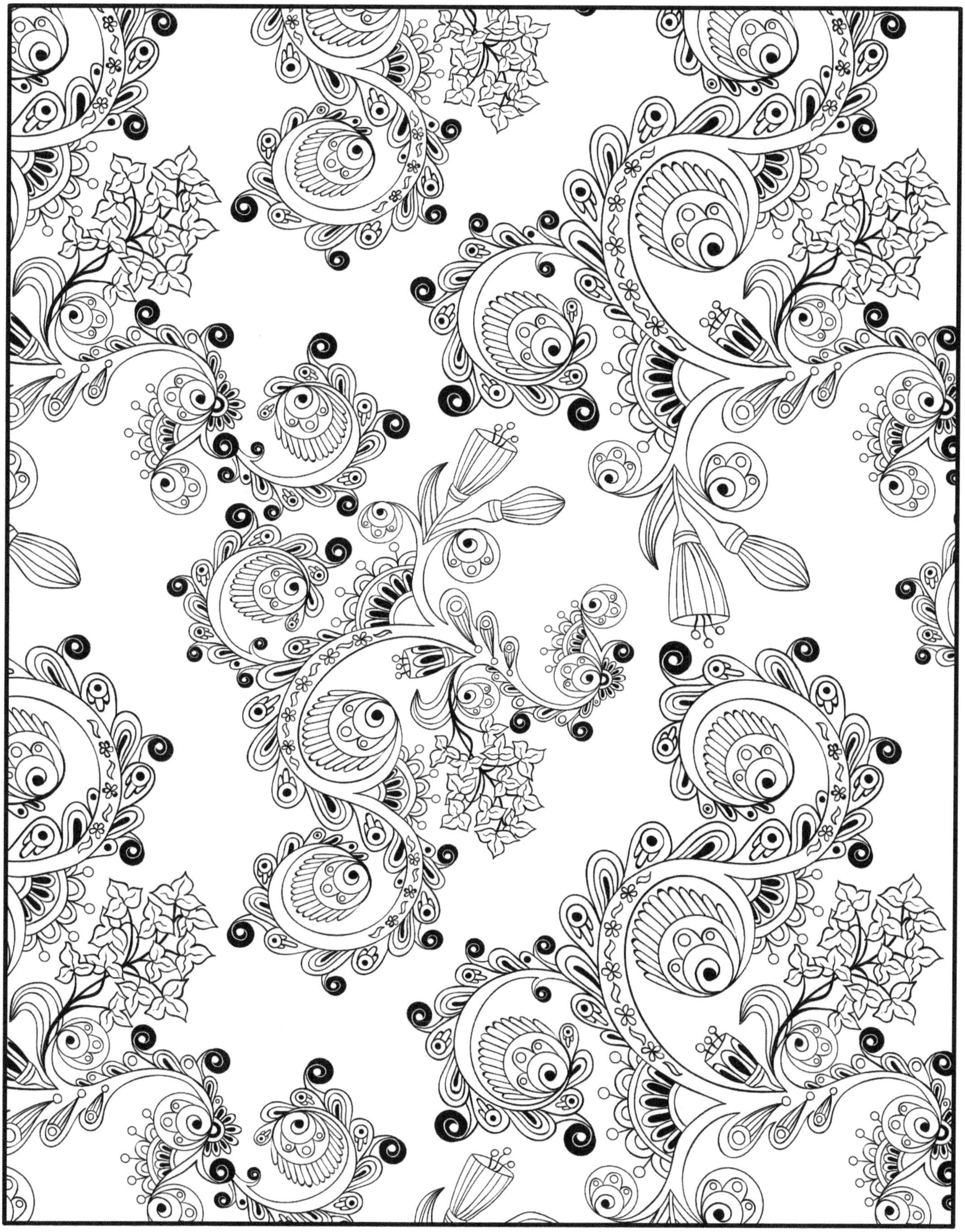

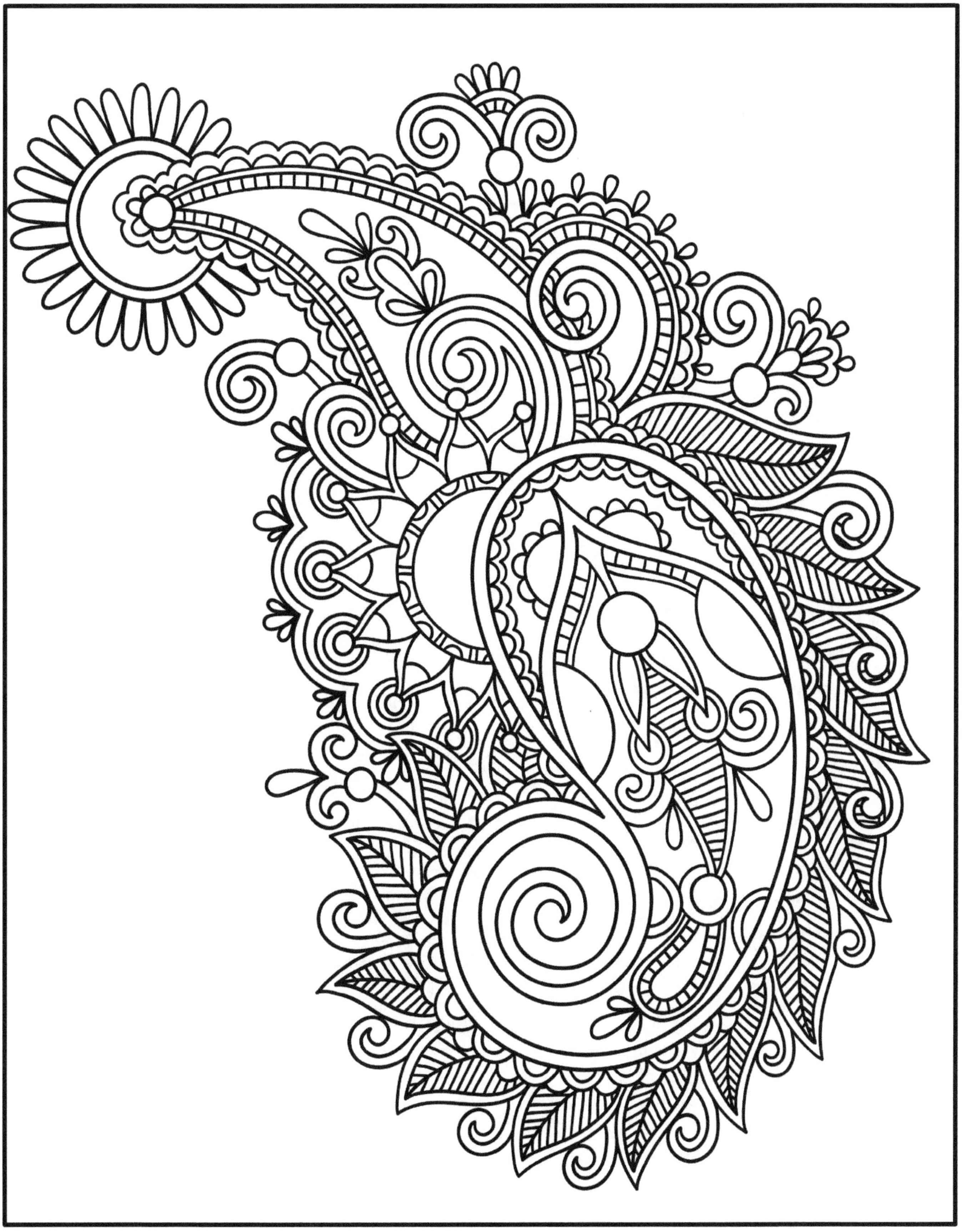

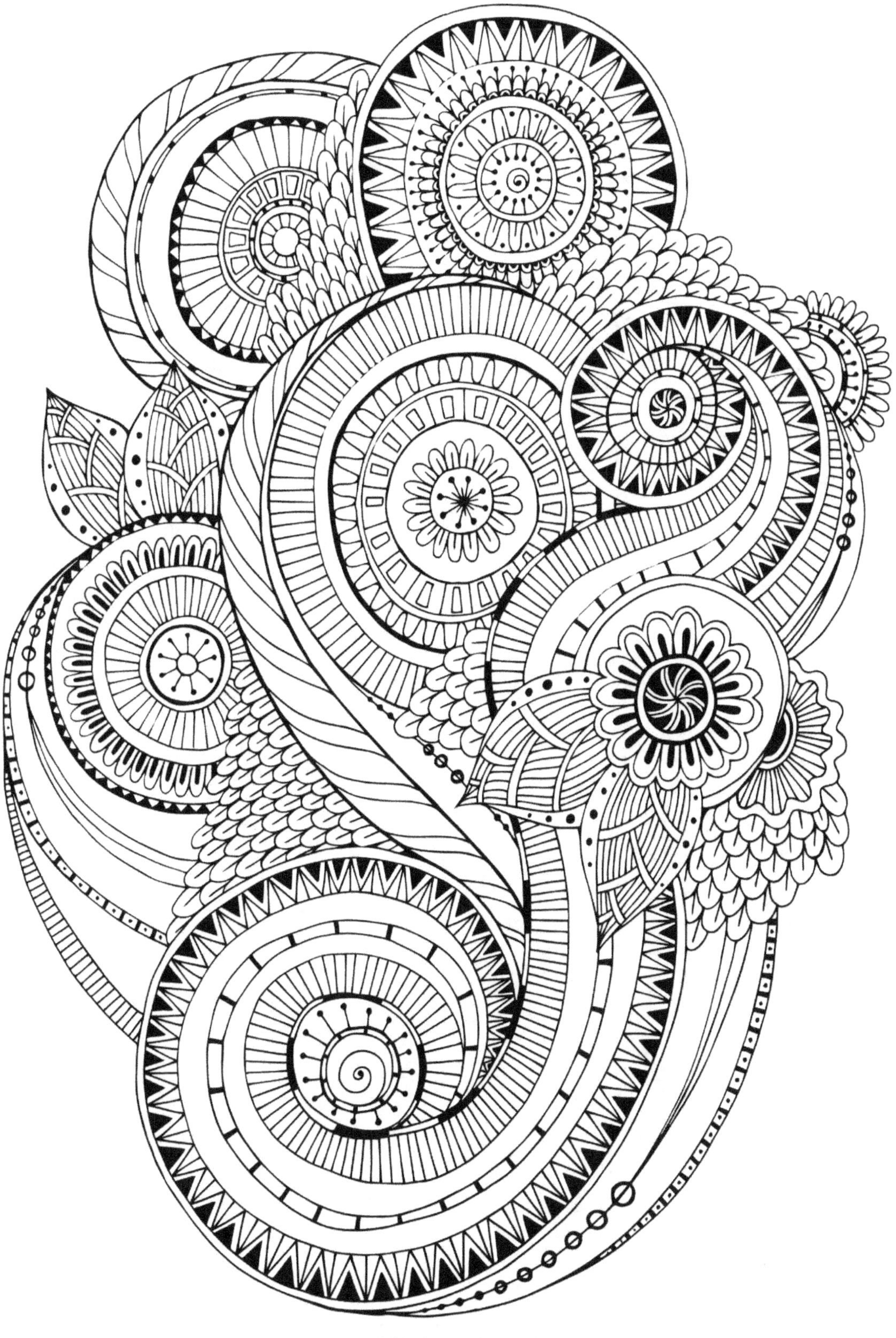

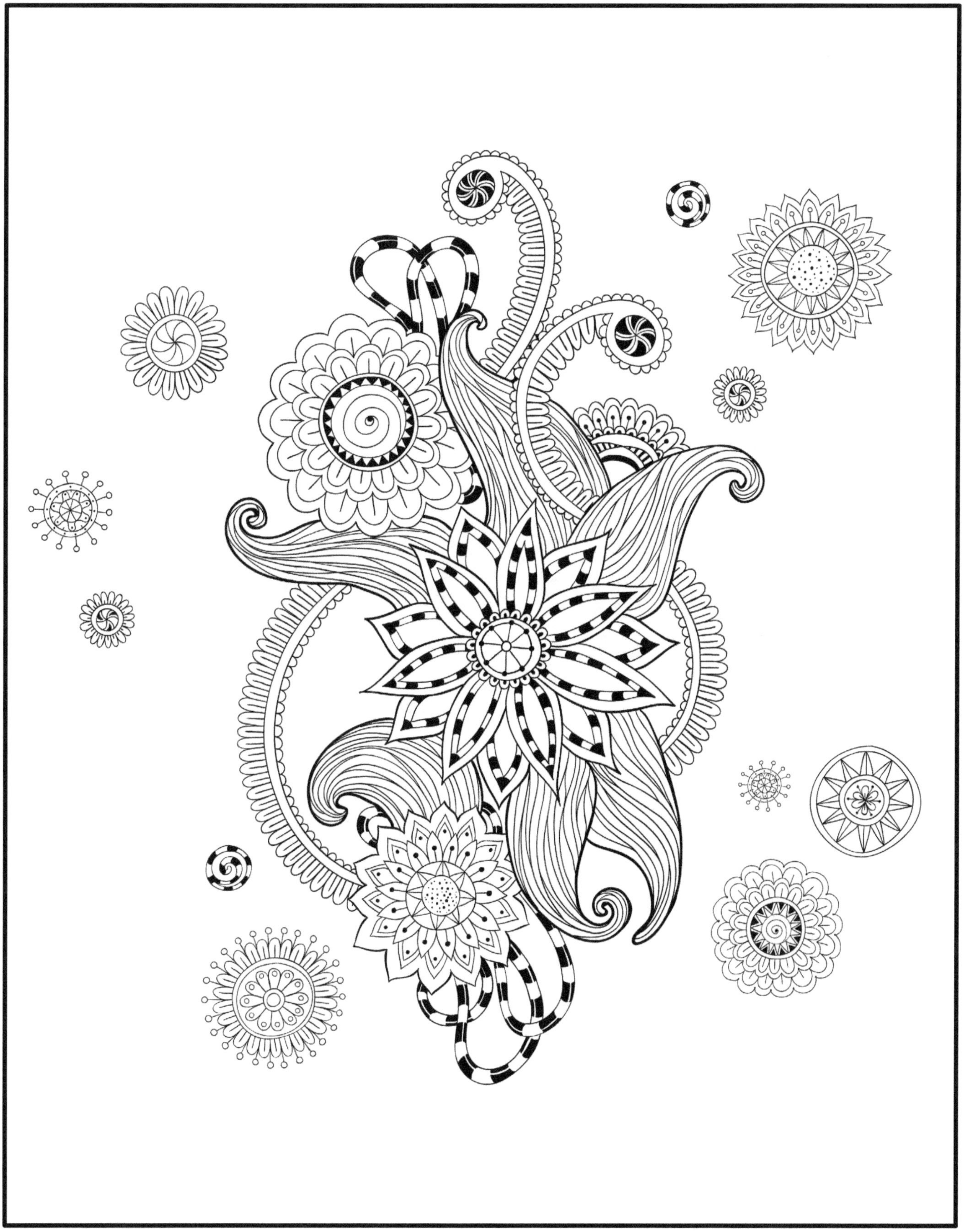

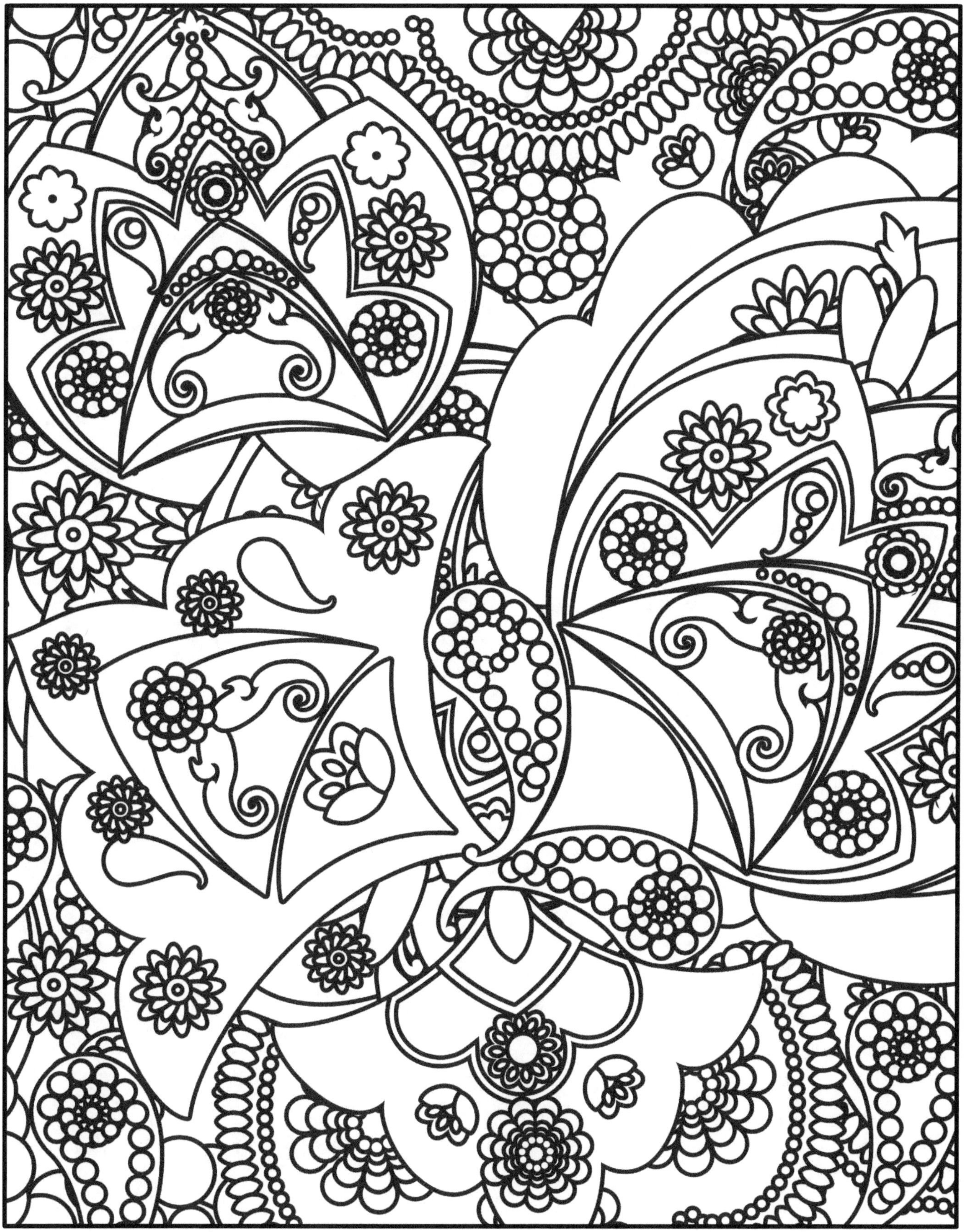

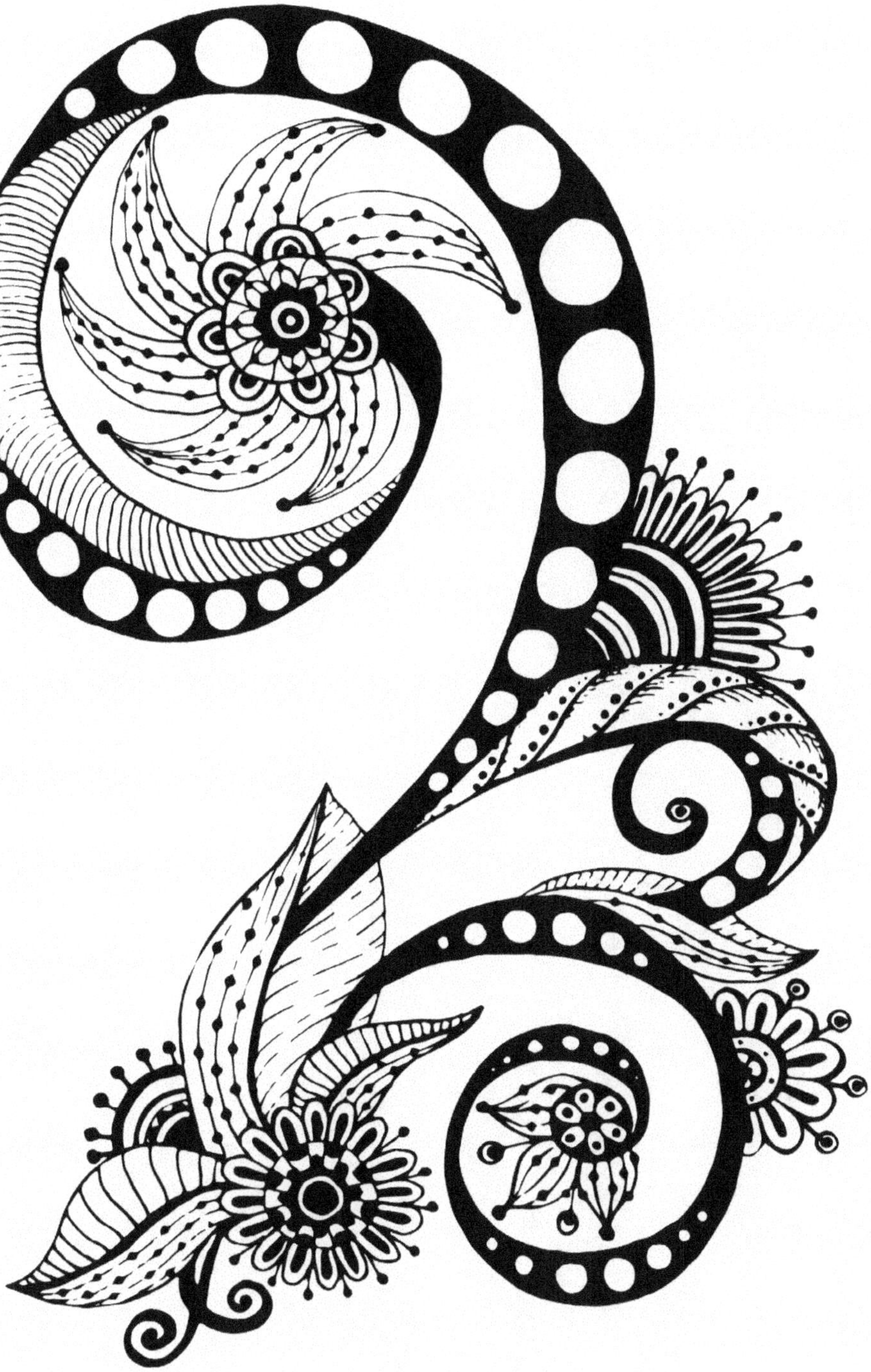

www.ingramcontent.com/pod-product-compliance
Lightning Source LLC
Chambersburg PA
CBHW080610190526
45169CB00007B/2960
* 9 7 8 1 5 3 4 9 8 6 8 4 8 *